Imperfect Paths

Creative Talents Unleashed

GENERAL INFORMATION

Imperfect Paths
By
Creative Talents Unleashed

1st Edition: 2016

This Publishing is protected under Copyright Law as a "Collection". All rights for all submissions are retained by the Individual Author and or Artist. No part of this publishing may be Reproduced, Transferred in any manner without the prior **WRITTEN CONSENT** of the "Material Owner" or it's Representative Creative Talents Unleashed.

www.ctupublishinggroup.com

Publisher Information
1st Edition: Creative Talents Unleashed
info@ctupublishinggroup.com

This Collection is protected under U.S. and International Copyright laws

Copyright © 2016: Creative Talents Unleashed

ISBN-13: 978-1-945791-03-1(Creative Talents Unleashed)
ISBN-10: 1-945791-03-9

$10.95

Credits

Book Cover

Raja Williams

Editors

Authors Responsible For Own Work

Foreword

Donna J. Sanders

Foreword

How many people can say they have not walked on rough terrain to get to where they are today? Most of us have been bruised and beaten to find out who we really are within; to find joy in this life we have been given. We are flawed beings with imperfect paths, and those turbulent journeys can either make us or break us.

It is easy to blame our past wrongs, the people who have tarnished our trust, and the bad bets the world throws at us. But we still hold the power to make a choice to become better than the humans who hurt us; to be the voice of change by learning from the experiences which have attempted to break us. Along the many roads traveled, the decisions we make will determine who we are to become.

Take a moment to walk in another's shoes. The poets here have opened their Pandora's Box, not to release the personal demons that taunt or once to keep them confined, but to share how to sever the weights one is shackled to.

Donna J. Sanders, *Author*

Table of Contents

Foreword   v
Donna J. Sanders

Stolen Time *Tony Hicks*	1
Whispers in the Shadows *Tony Hicks*	3
Quest *Sarah Lamar King*	5
Mirror *Sarah Lamar King*	6
Snow Globe (the Year of the Divorce) *Maureen Buckley*	7
The Weight of the World *Maureen Buckley*	9
I Clown *Don Beukes*	11
Emergence *Don Beukes*	12
Broken Mirror of Me *Baidha Fercoq*	14

Table of Contents

Courage   15
Baidha Fercoq

Shattered Heart   16
Neha Talwar Tandon

Spirit of Life   17
Neha Talwar Tandon

The Journey   18
Debasish Mishra

Living for Love   20
Amanda J. Evans

Imperfectly Perfect   22
Amanda J. Evans

AND SO   24
Elizabeth Deborah Cohen

Emptied   26
Brenda-Lee Ranta

Things I Would Say   28
Brenda-Lee Ranta

My Father's Son   31
Lynn White

Intertwined   33
Bonita Y. McCoy

Table of Contents

Job Satisfaction   34
Vincent Van Ross

The Inheritance   36
Teresa Roberts

Snobs and Swine   38
Heath Brougher

The Ingrate   39
Heath Brougher

Cancer   40
Brigitte Poirson

Disillusionment   41
Mark Andrew Heathcote

It's Just Hard Luck   42
Mark Andrew Heathcote

Suggestions   43
Paige Turner

Dilemma   44
YASHWANT KANODIA

December 20, 2011 - Real Life Event   45
Christena AV Williams

Mario Dean's Death - Causing a Revolution   46
Christena AV Williams

Table of Contents

Victory *Shirley Ann Cooper*	48
The Day I Had To Say Goodbye *Shirley Ann Cooper*	50
Ebb Tide *Edward Ahern*	52
God's New Clothes *Edward Ahern*	53
Defying Odds *Elizabeth Daniel*	54
They *Vee Townsend*	55
The Journey *Vee Townsend*	56
Hero *Krista S. Vowell- Clark*	57
I Am Not My Father *Raja Williams*	58
Buried Alive *Raja Williams*	60
Poster Children *Debra McLain*	61

Table of Contents

Euphoria   62
Debra McLain

A Mindless Patter   63
Ken Allan Dronsfield

Broken   64
Ameena K.G

Secrets   65
Valormore De Plume

Echoes From The Past Repeat   66
Valormore De Plume

Epilogue

The Starving Artist Fund   68

Our Links   70

Imperfect Paths

Creative Talents Unleashed

Stolen Time

I live deep in her shadow
walking just one step behind,
Kept safe by her unknowing
while living on her stolen time.

So, I wait alone in the darkness
waiting for you to steal time,
Time for love before you're missed
time to commit our old crime.

But you are so the master thief
spinning tales of an honest life,
Raising yet again my dying belief
of me as your good and loving wife.

But your tale's have grown thin
thin as my old maid's grey hair,
Leaving me with but stale sins
and her with such unknown cares.

Yet, I have played the worse part
believing your played out lies,
Giving them a warm truthful heart
as summer beneath her blue sky.

Imperfect Paths

So, now after all these stolen years
we must part only as friends,
Strange, how your love now sears
and I the one betrayed in the end.

But, only now at you're going
do my weeping red eyes see,
That the hours you were stealing
they were stolen all from me.

Tony Hicks

Whispers in the Shadows

Draw slowly that most bitter of blades
that cuts away the gentle bonds of love,
Oh stay the tempest of your burning rage
soften that iron hand in its velvet glove.

Fear to take that slow endless walk
deep into the silent gathering gloom,
Where the shadows of memories stalk
and midnight poisons the Sun at noon.

Flee the bold lie that sparks such hot fire
leaping to life so deeply in your breast,
Hold back bitter hate and your dreadful ire
let the baying hounds go find their rest.

Remember that not all who do so speak
will hold your honor in any high esteem,
No they are base liars softly they creep
silently they squirm wriggle and scheme.

Imperfect Paths

Happiest only in the miseries they make

counting out their success in your pain,

Glorying at your blind all-consuming hate

making it all too easy to win their game.

Instead place your trust in one you know

that loves without any base talk of cost,

Reach for them now before they do go

hold them so tight before they are lost.

Tony Hicks

Quest

Forged from oppression,

A revenant,

Credence on wings,

An alchemist.

Quest for lucidity,

In obscurities' reign,

My reflection,

This Cage only frees me.

Sarah Lamar King

Mirror

As I drown in ink, in secrecy,

A riven mind comes easily,

Amid your words of weaponry,

Unmask the ugliest side of me,

Willing poetry to speak my reality,

Hiding behind pages of elegies,

The dust of annotations and reverie,

Reflection atrophied.

Sarah Lamar King

Snow Globe (the Year of the Divorce)

Predictable pastoral setting, sharp unnatural trees
point upward to protect the tiny house with green shutters
encased in silence. Not serene in the real sense
but by all appearances stable. Cemented to the base,
so determined to keep a tight hold
on the fabricated foundation to which it clings

White plastic flakes coat the fake landscape and
lay undisturbed and unsuspecting.
Not pretty, but orderly and expected.

Until you pick us up and shake harder than I could
ever have thought you capable. Without warning
AN EXPLOSION!
I am sucked out of the resin-house window.

My head slams against the hard glass globe.
I am stunned – tumbling, spinning, frantic, flailing
my hands claw at nothingness.
I will my eyes blind then sputter scream, terrified.
My back cracks the ground my breath flattens.
I cannot breathe cannot think. Pain is everywhere.
I have never been so afraid.

I grab at grass but I am a bullet ricocheting.
I open my eyes to a blizzard swallowing me.
I strike smooth glass again this time with my face.
I am rabid; too terrified to think then the ground
reaches up to punch me and I crash on my butt.
First frantic glimpses of small familiarities whiz by
and I want to plan.

Imperfect Paths

Curled up, prenatal the next impact shudders through me.
I anticipate it and I am less off balance. Momentum shifts.
I begin to spin and turn with less chaos, stretching out,
eyes open wide I see my reflection in the cold glass an
instant before I smack the side.
This time I push off with my own power.

Steadily slowing I bounce and twirl – think angel wings.
I view my world from first way up high then way down
low. I spring and whirl and find the pace, tentative
acrobatic cartwheels, somersault, handstands, lazy
backstrokes I am getting the hang of this.
Fear has transformed into manic exhilaration.

This unknown becomes my known. The unexpected…
titillating. I surge. I flip. Equilibrium returns. I know
the silly satisfaction of moments with both feet on the
ground. I will myself to find my weight, recall my gravity.
Commanding myself back to the ground where I lay
Panting. Exhausted for sure, but triumphant!

To be expected, my world still shakes with
undulating ferocity, mostly slow rolls across smooth
surface – unsettling but not unkind. The other times with
more fierceness than I prefer. I revisit fear but recover more
quickly.

Is it crazy to admit that there are days, sometimes
when I shake the globe ever so slightly? I do this to remind
myself to kick off and away and to breathe.

Maureen Buckley

The Weight of the World

"I think they are pretty," I say
from my supplicant's pose.
Shaking my head, I finger tiny fuchsia flowers
nesting on lacy green leaves
soft as cotton to the touch

"Yeah, I know," you say,
as if one time too many.
"But they are weeds and will take over the garden."
You have personal knowledge
so I do not disagree.

I am a novice gardener lacking
any genuine enthusiasm.
I will trust it is necessary and I am determined
to do my part. Kneeling in the sandy soil
I commit to the rhythm I am creating

The roots release their hold so easily.
I also let down my guard,
"Is it a turn off for you that I have gained weight?"
I am alarmed I released this question
so irretrievably into the open spaces.

The silence before you speak stings
almost more than what you say:
"It is not NOT a turn off," you state
pragmatically then your words
sit leaden and naked between us in the stagnant air.

"Oh" I say, silly and embarrassed.
I sit back on my heels and allow the thickness of fatigue
to cover me like a warm blanket.

Imperfect Paths

I welcome the late afternoon light
swimming in my eyes.

I reach over and pluck a white dandelion,
fluffy and full-bodied and shake it
without much feeling.
The fibrous spears release into the air;
I watch as they catch the afternoon breeze
whisked away up and out until they disappear.

It would be nice to be able to do this.
I admit to myself as I gaze after the fragments
dancing and bouncing and floating off,
no longer earthbound – instead
giddy and free
and light as a feather.

Maureen Buckley

I Clown

Early childhood development
quite a daunting predicament,
Surrounded and protected by
adults – My sentinels elected,
No young minds to play with
or close friends to stay with –
My eyes observed the culture
of the era – Music blasting from
Abba and the eternal love from
a loving adopted mamma.

Early school days a nervous affair,
Comparing my lightly coloured curly
hair – Surveying my surroundings
with a nervous stare – Even my voice
was not always clear, hiding my insecure
fragile veneer – Bullies mocked sniggered
and sneered, exposing emotions most feared.

Teenage moments brought conflicting
components – Identity crises became my
inflicting nemesis – What to say how to
speak when to speak, calming my inner
freak – My forced smile masking my daily
inner grime – My inner clock sounding an
ominous constant chime.

I wore my expected social cloak – The daily drown of me –

For I am clown…

Don Beukes

Emergence

The loss of a dear one
a crippling feeling – You
crawl in the aftermath
ready to fall – Dark
thoughts shroud your
vision, your essence
drowning in a sympathy
crowning.

Your thoughts swirling
catapulting in a bottomless
abyss – The missing a daily
confessing of unsaid things,
The gems shared – Love once
used to bring.

Avoid this nowhere road
toxic void – Allow yourself to
hear the flapping of wings
speaking of future bright things –
Take a deep slow breath out of the
clutches of a living death.

Let your nerve endings ignite
once again loving feelings
for those left behind – Read once
again their outpouring of love
and promises of all things kind.

Smell once again familiar

Imperfect Paths

scents in a shared aromatic garden,
Let your fingers dig yet again to
plant poignant memories once again –
Your spiritual healing a necessary
urgence – For your renewed

liberating emergence.

Don Beukes

Personal traumas play a large role in ultimately defining a person. While the journey can be long and for some it never ends, individually we seek to make sense of their meaning. For some, the weight of past traumas is insurmountable and for others the burdens seem a slight affair. This poem reflects upon the personal journey of self-examination and suggests self-love and understanding are vital aspects of healing and accepting the cumulative picture of who we are.

Broken Mirror of Me

I did not know
I could not see
the fractured pictures
of hidden me.
I tried so hard
to hold together
the pieces of me
I wanted to be.
I did not know
I could not see
the fractured pieces
I had to be.
I see me now
no harsh of tone
I understand
the strength it took.
Now I know
I clearly see
the fractured pieces
I call them me.

Baidha Fercoq

There stands no one in the whole of Earth that will never contend with deepest sorrows. And in theses sorrows are often born the metal of man. This poem speaks to such moments of courage that often define our greatest personal victories when we chose to stand strong and hold onto hope.

Courage

It is found in the moment of choice
when we alone are called to stand
and declare to all the road we take
when faded promises reveal themselves.
Echoed voices strain to cheer
"Do the best you can
with what you have."
But it is easy to succumb
and grieve with salted tear
imaginary hopes that speak
"It could have been so dear."
All must close with sorrows of theirs
for the ground is deeply layered
endless fragments of faded promises.
Let not surrender claim your hope
lift your head and raise your eyes
for courage is born in moments of choice.
When one allows faded promises
to become the ground upon which
tomorrow's joy will stand.

Baidha Fercoq

Shattered Heart

I am shattered from deep within.
The thought of one that made my smile wide,
Now narrows down on just a thought of his perspective towards my life.
I am shattered from deep within.

I cried on his shoulders,
For nothing but some support.
But in return, my faith was ruined,
With his entire mighty jolt.
I am shattered from deep within.

I thought, his love was mine,
But was nothing more than an insecure gesture.
I was heading along with him towards my dreams,
But realized lately,
That he was the one to fade them completely.
I am shattered from deep within.

The trust again, will never be gained.
It was a fairy tale, which will never be accomplished again.
I am shattered from deep within.

Neha Talwar Tandon

Spirit of Life

I woke up early today,
Because it was important.
To wish her the day,
Hoping she finds her gift significant.

Last night,
When clock struck twelve.
I hurriedly ran in the twilight,
To ask the stars for her longer survive.

She was under dejection,
With her life.
But her art never went under suppression,
Although it came out to be stronger and fine.

I held her hand,
Tight enough, not to let her go.
And kissed her band,
Which I had tied years ago.

Our friendship means a lot,
It is a strong bond of trust.
My prayers for her are on every dot,
We have built this relation from crust.

I wished her good day,
With wishes filled in my arms.
Hope she conquers the world someday,
And her lost smile arrives with a charm.

Neha Talwar Tandon

The Journey

It was a shaky start
Of a momentous journey,
I wobbled like an acrobat
Walking on a slender rope
In the circus.

They doubted my skills,
My decisions,
They had a problem
With everything I did!
Like foes armed with arrows,
They attacked me with question marks--
How? Why? What?

I followed my heart blindly,
Chasing the tantalizing dreams.
I was tired, tried and tested,
But never did I think to give up!
I battled against the obstinate odds,
The twists and twirls of Fate,
The irrevocable pace of Time
And the pressure of hostile adversity.

It was a thorny path indeed,
A road of trials and tribulations,
A passage of loss and pain.

Like a much-awaited dawn,
I reached the gateway of prosperity
Where doors of auspiciousness
Ushered in the light and aroma
Of a beautiful future.
Success and prosperity

Imperfect Paths

Trickled alongside like morning dew.
Ah! It was a hectic journey
That culminated with fruition,
A journey of tests and triumphs,
The very journey of life!

Debasish Mishra

Living for Love

I've felt the pain of death.
The cold touch it leaves upon your soul.
The fear of pain so great
I was afraid to live.
Alone and tortured
I became its tasty treat.
Smarties, easily swallowed whole,
yet it savoured me.
Allowing my pain to last, melting slowly
in its pit of despair.
Like a dose of dental anesthetic
Death left me numb to life.
Its crippling agony returning unannounced
no dental work complete.

I feared love, a reminder of the black shadow
that longed to consume me.
But love found me.
It waited on the top of a mountain
too steep to climb without a rope,
a rope that dangled in front of me like a carrot.

Your smiles a ray of warmth, like a sun
breaking free on a summers day.
I'd smile back,
and death would remind me of the
storms that it could rage
But you kept smiling.
Breaking through the clouds,
daring me to grab that rope,
while death stood with its knife waiting,
to sever the bond.

Imperfect Paths

I climbed slowly, one step at a time.
Reaching for the summit, my sunshine,
my sanctuary.
I stumbled as rain battered my mind
casting memories of pain in sharp
frenzied lightning strikes.

Your presence became my umbrella, transparent
allowing sunlight to filter through

I made it to the top of that mountain,
to a love so patient, it endured all.
And now I live.
I live in love,
knowing Death will come
But I will no longer be its tasty treat

Amanda J. Evans

Imperfectly Perfect

I'm fat. I'm dumpy
Rejected by society.
For not fitting the standards.

Not 5 foot 6, nor 34C, or D, or E,
Just A – below average.

Not size 0, or 2, or 4, or 6, or 8
I'm 12 – Too big to be perfect.

My locks don't shine or curl.
My eyebrows aren't HD.
I don't contour,
or dress to conform.
I'm an outcast in a society dominated by perfection

Perfection garnered from software
that erases individuality,
removing so called flaws.
Sun kissed freckles and stretch marks,
Signifiers of joy and motherhood.
Rounded bellies no good either,
You're not supposed to enjoy good food.
Grey that signifies age and wisdom,
A definite no for society's perfection.

I don't fit on your perfect scale,
Size 12, 36A, five foot, with
sun kissed freckles and non-penciled eyebrows.
I don't hide my skin behind layers of makeup.
I'm me, a normal woman striving to fit
into a society beholden to editing software
and what sells magazines.

Imperfect Paths

I'm not perfect by your socialist standards and yet,
I'm still beautiful, I'm still me,
in this world obsessed by a perfection
created by imperfect ideals.

Amanda J. Evans

AND SO

I became determined to
love the smell of things
gone wrong.
To find their beauty,
their broken vacuum cleaner hearts.

A bad carburetor
smells of summer's bloom, and heat.
A broken marriage
has the scent of over cooked meat
and wilted flowers that never mended
anything

I loved those flowers anyway
and the roots that brought them
up from ground
and the seed packages
with their artistic renditions
and the water they drank all summer
from the hose.

I learned to recycle
arguments into strawberry plants
Took a string of betrayals
and stitched a quilt

I could sew broken
promises into patches
for my jacket.
Your favorite vase
shattered
became a mosaic for the bathroom.
I made a lantern of a few old lies

Imperfect Paths

someone told
and was grateful for the light
it lent to the path through
the woods
to my studio of ailments
and the off brand hate
that had been tossed my way

That is where I go now to manufacture
various iridescent miracles
I take a handful
each day of the newly sprouted ones
and spread them around
and around the yard
and down, down come the birds

Elizabeth Deborah Cohen

Emptied

Praying to the ceiling, she begged for death,
then remembering the little people across the hall,
she agreed to go on.

Fists banging on steering wheels
Rage spewing spittle onto her face
Keys thrown at stairwells
Doors slamming shut repeatedly
Constant scowling, sarcastic words
Children scattering like leaves in a wind storm
Complaints about the weather, the food, the shopping.
Bigoted hatred, comments about fat people, slow people.
Pulsing temples, knit brows, tightened lips
Demanding respect, demanding quiet, demanding
Self-righteous indignation, sneering
Laughing at her, demeaning her thoughts

She died to herself, all dreams withering,
her mind became muddled like scrambled eggs,
left on a plate overnight.

Curses so loud, they travelled to the heavens;
yelling at the television; litanies of expletives
dishes on floors, beside crumpled chip bags
Flicking lights off and on while she bathed
Howling through the door when she quietly sang
Deeming her choices to be "fucking junk!"
Children being chastised for sitting on sofas
Emptying cupboards, to make them rewash every plate
Seated in his chair, admonishing her till the sun rose
Screaming at the children for practicing their dance steps

Holding doors closed so that she could not escape

Imperfect Paths

Shoving her against walls, his fingers buried in her arms
She pictured him dead if she couldn't die first,
she snickered at his cheap apologies
hearing white noise in her brain.

Looking at her through the screen door
Calm.. ice cold inside.. she stood
mouthing words he couldn't believe
Screaming, chaos, running up the stairs
Suitcases, boxes, clothing being packed
Following her from room to room
Lips moving angrily, his guttural sounds
Pleading, crying, threatening, continuous motion
Footsteps up and down stairwells
Frenzy, panic, pure mayhem and chaos
Calmly standing her ground; her eyes deadened
Terror filling his face, his loss of control

Pulling out of the driveway, never looking back;
she felt nothing, with nothing left to lose
left to find everything...

Whatever everything was...

Brenda-Lee Ranta

Things I Would Say

*I arrived into this world
in perfection;
as all babies arrive
Time taints perception
Time taints perfection*

*Deep longing to heal
my ruminations;
experiences created
Time taints perception
Time taints perfection*

My sweet little self with your yellow hair and periwinkle eyes; in all innocence of being in the joy of existence, I speak in earnest, with the wisdom of age

Daddy died. He did not abandon you; his agreement with the universe was exist here, long enough to create you. He has loved you that much.

Children do not invite sexual acts upon them. You were never sullied, therefore little one, do not spend your life scrubbing away the acts of another.

Judgement is subjective. Do not dance on the stage of public opinion to determine your worth When you give your power away to another, the result is fear.

Imperfect Paths

If you choose another out of loneliness, you shall never satisfy your desires. Only you have the ability to heal what is broken within you; be your first love.

Never measure your value or another's value by physical appearance. In the long-term, it is the soul that will love you and your soul that loves. The rest returns to the earth.

Every time your heart breaks, it leaves behind a lesson. Get out of victim-hood, forgive others, forgive yourself.
It is then that you will overcome insecurity and derisiveness.

You are worthy of love with a great capacity to love. Dry your eyes and smile, for one day you will hold your children in your arms and discover unconditional love.

Never fitting in with the fray is not a fault, it is who you are. Solitude may become you, bringing you solace. Let it be a time of contemplation and creativity for your soul.

For every action there is a consequence. Be ready to accept it, good or bad, it was your path to

Imperfect Paths

follow. Make peace with yourself; accept who you are fully.

One day you will stop living in the fear of being hurt. You will set healthy boundaries, allowing yourself to truly love and be truly loved; which is your true purpose.

You were always loved little one; for you are one with all that is and all that will be. This is but a temporary journey to rid your soul of that which never served you.

I pen this love letter
of conciliation;
Time eliminates perception
Time recreates perfection

Brenda-Lee Ranta

My Father's Son

I never knew
my father's son.
Even though
I met him once,
or maybe twice,
I never knew him.

And then I met
his son.
Caught him
miraculously
in a net.
Held on to him
tightly.

And, I found
that he hadn't left early,
my father's son.
He'd waited for me,
wondering,
for a long time.

And so I found him,
my father's son.
When he was
just ninety six,
I found him.
But I was too late
to know him.

Imperfect Paths

At ninety five,
he was already dead.
So I never knew him,
my father's son.

Lynn White

- *First published in Scarlet Leaf Review, May 2016*

Intertwined

Birth and death, they intertwine
Like vines upon an arbor.
They ring about the structure of life
They keep us humble and somber.
There cannot be one without the other
They cannot exist apart.
They ring around the human soul
They tear then mend the heart.
Birth and death, they intertwine
Like gardens gone astray.
They ring about our daily world
They give and take away.
There must be death for birth to rise
One grows out of the other.
They ring around our very being
We glory, and we suffer.
Birth and death, they intertwine
Uncontrolled by man.
One where we are going,
And one where we began.
The two cannot be parted
They share a common thread.
It is the act of living
By which birth and death are fed.
So comes now every man
From birth to death to trod,
And the life that thrives between
Is our testimony to God.

Bonita Y. McCoy

Job Satisfaction

Life does not offer
Too many options—
Opportunities restrict
The pleasures of Life

When we are in search
Of suitable opportunities
At the beginning of our career
We hardly have any options

I wanted to be a writer
But, the need for money,
Forced me take up the first job
That came my way

I never found there
What I always wanted
All I found was a steady flow
Of income that kept me going

I was doing a regular job
Picking up a monthly salary
I had some little job security
But, no job satisfaction

I was clear about my destination
But, my car seemed to have
Veered off in a different direction
Away from my true destiny

So, after thirty years
Of administrative work
I quit my job one day

Imperfect Paths

And, took to writing

Now, I write when I like
I do whatever I feel like
The fund flow is erratic
But, I really love what I do

Vincent Van Ross

The Inheritance

Winter always reminds her
of the fragility of loneliness
It sweeps in on the wings
of birds that have the intestinal fortitude
to sing in spite of icy winds
carrying a bitter sting.

She wasn't particularly tough though
Piling on warm clothes, she'd shiver
by the fire with pots of tea while
her thoughts strayed to darker days
Lost to the world for a while
Unable to deliver a single smile

Folks said that she shouldn't care
after the passing of so many years
Let it go, shed your tears, and let it go
And, when the sun was shining,
she could let it go, well, not entirely
but at least attain a loosened grip
letting it slip away

Is that cheating, she wondered out loud,
to pretend that the dark days before
she had her freedom to fly
no longer obscured a sunny sky?

Oh, those persistent memories
Buried in her genes
A sexually transmitted family pain
Intertwined with a thread of consciousness
that she continually fought to regain

Imperfect Paths

Yes, the years have passed so quickly
She's no longer that young girl who yearns
Except on occasion when those winter days
return…

Teresa Roberts

Snobs and Swine

Their nails-on-chalkboard voices
filled the halls. Every day, I'm,
walking through their swarms,
was drowned by a sea of snootiness and conformity,
invective and thoughtlessness and yuppie echoes
and mirrorism and insult and swine-talk.
Year after year I was subject
to their condescension, the self-made pedestal of ego
from which they shouted down at me,
throwing spears of jagged jibes. Their voices irked:
phony voices annoyed, saturated in selfishness,
became the world, became my routine.
My life growing dimmer by the second,
caked in the snobby twang of their venomous valley-girl and
boy voices.

To this day I'd like to throw their bodies and actions
on the white picket fences of suburbia
that doubtlessly ran along their front yards.

Heath Brougher

The Ingrate

I have mangled certain paths laid out before me.
Paths that appeared sometimes abruptly, sometimes not,
laden with only good intention, sprawling out
with only nothing other than wide benefit to offer.

I have ruined these roads,
damaged them with a crooked and careless walk.

Random relative presents bestowed
routes of benevolent aberration and a safe escape.
A trail to easily gallop through summer
and come out sunny on the other side.

Somehow I failed these lucky paths,
and tarnished these gorgeous selfless gifts.

I offer a sorrowed apology
for my usual reckless trampling. An apology
for my actions of not cherishing and of taking for granted
these long-stretching roads of help.

The high sun could have been clasped
and held close to the heart, finally bringing light to such a
darkly place.
This path of tedium and suffering could have been quit
for a favorable one strewn with brighter lights and better
intentions.

I never meant to be so cold and distant,
but being the ingrate I am, I was.

Heath Brougher

Cancer

Stamped, stomped, stultified.

"Heal? I doubt you can, sir.
You've got cancer."

They will cleanse your nose,
Slit your throat,
Burn your bones,
instill vitriol into your veins
From their cans, sir.
But you are a prisoner
Of your own cells.

"Kill it?
Nothing we can, sir."

Cure yourself, if you can, sir.

"But can, sir,
Cancer
Be healed?"

"Maybe a serial phraser
And a metalover
Could ignite your spirit
And consume all your metastases…"

"Then with their love and words,
I can, sir,
Heal from cancer."

Brigitte Poirson

Disillusionment

You can paint the skies and make a rainbow
But you cannot quieten a dark rainstorm
Not when it's political when it's the norm,
Those people will rise up, they'll refuse to bow.
As long as we are speaking; we are friends
Love is a fellowship at times ours is-
A sinking ship with bilge water to pump out
But like matchwood we always seem to float.
But if they sink my small boat or your boat
There'll be no brotherhood no love of man
Yes, they can paint the skies and make us vote!
But when it's over this shit will hit the fan.

Mark Andrew Heathcote

It's Just Hard Luck

The face of poverty is here again
The silent vagrant without a friend
Sits cross-kneed watching business men
In suits and ties condescend-
Their needs, filling pockets out of greed
They aren't moved by the homeless
They all stand together, black-millipede
Looking at you like you're dead begonias.
They aren't bothered that your livelihood
Was destroyed, they made a fast buck
Let's not kid ourselves theirs no brotherhood
When they look at you, it's just hard luck.
Oh, and if you're lucky they might just put
A few old silver coins in your flannel cap
Maybe enough to feed that bed companion
That sad old greyhound dog sat on your lap
Have a nice day, sir! Don't forget to come back.

Mark Andrew Heathcote

Suggestions

He suggested I wear more vibrant colors
He doesn't like seeing me in dark colors

He suggested I wear Mascara
He thought my eyes would be prettier

He suggested I wear high heels and a dress
He wants to see me be more womanly

He suggested I wear lipstick
He wants to kiss my pretty lips

He suggested I send him nude pictures
He wants to see my naked body

He suggested I call him more
He wants to hear my voice

He suggested I listen more
He thinks I don't hear him

He suggested I be his woman
He must be crazy . . .

He suggests I become someone else.

Paige Turner

Dilemma

There I am standing on the cliff
Lost in a dilemma
whether to wrestle or slide
as I see the light thinning
I scrutinize the life of my brothers
the brothers from different mothers
some at the peak of their success
others whining over the intricacies of life
and there were few like me standing on the cliff
Drowning in the dilemma
Dilemma of life
We all know what is right and what's not
but sometimes you tangle
the moment when I finally decided to go for it
the face of my love flickered at my sight
Holy shit I just can't give up on her
What about the promises I made
What about the times when I wished
For her smile, for her happiness
It was then when I decide
If it's for her, I will the walk extra miles
Harder than anyone could
Because no one could ever love her more than i do
Yes I do and I will do whatever it takes
Till my last breath
I welcome life with opens arms
It can try to rip me apart
But I am on my way out through
the dilemma to hit the highest point

YASHWANT KANODIA

December 20, 2011 - Real Life Event

Do I fear death?
Death was before me
Gripped
Counting seconds of my life
There I was facing judgment
Like votes in a ballot
Was I to live or die?
Cash pot and lucky five
Could not save me
All I Got was God watching me
My heart pounding
But still, I was calm
Not fearful
But wondering
What my end was to be
And finally,
When the gun man got what
He wanted
I could see fear in his eyes
His voice Tremble
He only took vanity
And left me with the greatest Gift,
Life on December 20, 2011.

Christena AV Williams

Mario Dean's Death - Causing a Revolution

I could not believe when I heard it on the news
That you were locked up for a spliff,
A misdemeanor
Before your mother could bail you
Emergency
She found you beaten, unblemished and left in a coma.

The message that is been sent by the authorities
Not that I condone breaking the law
However do not be caught smoking or in possession
Of Marijuana
A God made herb
However, you can smoke in the confinements of home a cigarette
Which in long term puncture your lungs
Bore holes in your windpipe
Hey, what is up with that?

I heard you died, the so call police justice con forum they
could not tell it straight
Did you die from falling off a bunk bed?
Beaten by inmates or by cops
Which is the story?
However, from what many speculate of who perpetuate
The suspects considered seems hazy
I personally do not pick sides
I am for justice does not matter whom it serves as long it is
served honestly.

However, one wonders why this kid was locked up
For a misdemeanor

Imperfect Paths

Denied bail
Found dead
Claimed to be without scratches
Is it psychologically or professionally done?
Was it arranged now blamed by the mute and deranged?
I blame the system
I blame us
We never stood up when our rights were violated
We stood by and became voiceless
Hopeless
We allowed it to reach thus far
We cry has if it was sudden
As if we did not know this day was coming
We forget things so easily
Nine-day wonder
Politicians jumping on this to score extra votes
Who sees the illusions?
Locked in manipulation
While many so call justice groups are missing in action
This is beyond murder, brutality and spliff
It is a bunch of things fused with aggression
A reflection of us as a society and people
Therefore, the temperature rises
I feel the tension and I know
It is coming
This is the spark for a revolution.

Christena AV Williams

Victory

He crawls through muddy waters trying to embrace,
A life he never wanted to face.
The wealth he works so hard to make,
Wasn't at all what he wanted to take.
He had a family that needed him so much,
He was their golden touch.
His work was filled with blood and toil,
Working from the soil.
Words fall short in times like these,
All he had were his knees.
Crying out to God for a favored plan,
The suffering he couldn't understand.
Why was everyone else going fast?
Yet his strength couldn't last.
His children cried out his name,
Daddy I'm so happy you came.
Our home is lost without you here,
When you stand close we never fear.
Our hungry bellies depend on you,
Because daddy's like you are few.
Even when you're tired and broken down,
We need you all around.
Soon he realized as God's plan unfolds,
There's a story untold.
While the struggle calls us to persevere,
We are made strong when faith is clear.
Believing that through this plan,
Above there are greater hands.
Now the challenge begins at last,
His change is growing fast.
He's learned that yesterday is completely gone,
But his victory is through but one.
The root of weakness that once grew,

Imperfect Paths

Made him the man his family knew.
While for others misery is bliss,
The victory is his.

Shirley Ann Cooper

The Day I Had To Say Goodbye

You were the hero in this little girl's heart,
Until the day you fell apart.
You gave me everything I needed most,
From my first guitar to my first home.
A bedroom set fit for a Princess or a Queen,
You were every little girl's dream.
The man who cried when I felt pain,
How I wish your heart would beat again.
I remember family vacations and parties too,
Things were right when I was with you.
It broke my heart to watch you fight,
A battle that wasn't right.
To watch you go from giving to needing,
With the sound of machines and tube feeding.
I wasn't prepared to watch you die,
I needed so badly to just cry.
The memories of you talking,
The life you knew while walking.
It all seemed so bitter sweet,
As I lotioned up your feet.
You no longer moved on your own,
Nor did you speak of home.
It was as if you weren't there,
It was a pain I just couldn't bare.
I sat by the phone waiting for your call,
But that didn't happen at all.
Your eyes were filled with emptiness,
To others peace and rest.
But for me it was a long and winding road,
A denial in my soul.
You didn't live in there anymore,
It was a stranger's door.
The man I use to know had drifted away,

Imperfect Paths

He just wasn't the same.
Then finally the call came through,
But it wasn't you.
A woman's voice spoke gently into my ears,
The words I dreaded to hear.
Your father went home and in peace at last,
But I still wonder, why so fast?
I never got the chance to hold you one last time,
To let you know you were the hero in my life.
The day you left my soul grew cold,
Remembering the new and old.
As time stood still, my heart just died,
But I conquered and revived.
Through all these trials I'd overcome,
You taught me more than anyone.
Today I can smile as I go on,
Defeat is crushed and gone.
I've learned a lesson through your eyes,
The day I had to say good bye.

Shirley Ann Cooper

Ebb Tide

Sometimes my low tides drop me
onto rocks and sharp edges.
coated with the seaweed rot
of decomposing failures
and littered with the broken shells
of promises unkept.
But in time, always,
the flood tide surges
washing clean my feet
and carrying me onward.

Edward Ahern

God's New Clothes

So little left of the old garments.
The fewer and older priests
face us robed in apologies.
Shrill tailors of God's message.
Costumed nuns have died away
replaced by off the rack laity.

The churning suits and dresses
That draped across the pews
have worn thin and sparse.
Churches are cast off
Like Good Will overcoats.
And strictures are raggedly observed.

Yet some of us still wear faith,
Displaying hand-me-downs in a church
no longer fashionable.
We're not dressed as we were,
and unsure of holy style,
but hopeful of our future ensemble.

Edward Ahern

Defying Odds

She'll never walk,
Speak her first word,
Better off in an institution,
That's what her mother heard,
And that's if she makes it,
If,
Emergency surgeries,
A hope and a prayer,
That in the morning,
She'd still be there,
That mother took her home,
Showered love like rain,
There we're plenty of hurdles,
Rough patches,
Too many to explain,
So many times,
They gave that little girl no chance,
But despite the odds,
She rewrote her own story,
No matter the circumstance,
Now she's about to turn 34,
Something that most thought she'd never see before,
Thanks to God and family,
That sassy little gal is me.

Elizabeth Daniel

They

They tell her she can't
She'll show them she can
They tell her she "Isn't"
She'll show them she "Is"

They've tried to push her down
She keeps rising
They've tried to hold her back
She keeps coming

You're not good enough
You're not strong enough
You're not smart enough
To them...she's deaf, blind and dumb

But SHE knows she can
SHE knows who she is
SHE is more than good enough
Stronger than they are
Smarter than they'll ever be

SHE is a survivor...and that's something THEY will never understand!

Vee Townsend

The Journey

In the middle of chaos
she hopes
In the middle of hoping
she dreams

Through all the struggles
the blood, the sweat and tears
she is forever seeking
she seeks that which has been denied her.

She longs for peace
she hopes for joy
she dreams of forever
she seeks a brighter tomorrow

Don't pity her
she neither needs nor wants it
don't ever think her weak
she's survived more than you can know.

Don't stand in her way
her journey won't allow it
but if you'll walk with her a while
she'll show you what love looks like.

Vee Townsend

Hero

The years have passed so quickly,
Since you left me standing here.
What happened to you, Daddy?
You traded my love,
For the taste of beer.
Your addiction led your life,
And suddenly, you were alone.
Your drinking destroyed us all,
And kept our house from being a home.
Only tears can find me now,
As I seek help, from powers that be.
I remember as a family,
We gathered by the lake.
To swim, ski and picnic,
Until the dawn would break.
Proud am I, of what you're life,
Turned out later, to be.
You became my HERO, Daddy,
The day you set the alcohol free.
I will always be your Little Princess,
Even though, you've gone away.
Heaven is your home now,
And in my heart, you'll stay.

Krista S. Vowell- Clark

I Am Not My Father

As I watched him walk away,
I realized the burdens he has carried
He carries with him;
His father's sins

They are attached to his soul
And anchored into his DNA

He walks like his father
He talks like his father
His angry outbursts performed;
Just like his father

In my own moments of anger
I accusingly yell out
"You're just like your dad,
why would you want to be like that?"

The silence cuts with a knife
His stare;
Kills me dead where I stand

That was the last time I saw him
He walked out the door;
His last words . . .

"I am not my father"

Imperfect Paths

Three days later . . .
He died of a drug overdose
He Died;
Just like his father.

Raja Williams

- *First Publication, Imprints In The Sand – published by Creative Talents Unleashed*

Buried Alive

With each and every passing thought,
I was slowly dying . . .
Under the refuse of other people's

**OPINIONS,
PREJUDICES,
AND PREFERENCES,**

I was entombed
Expectations of society
Buried me alive

Raja Williams

- *First Publication, Imprints In The Sand – published by Creative Talents Unleashed*

Poster Children

Homeless and hungry,
a campfire to keep us warm.
There were no make-believe tales,
of boogeymen hiding in the dark.
We were the main characters,
in a story of unfortunate events.
Living out of a station wagon,
there was no money for rent.
Often, we went without,
no water to scrub us clean.
Sometimes, there were days,
when we bathed in a stream.
Weeks turned into months,
we survived without beds.
Poster children for poverty,
with no roof over our head.

Debra McLain

Euphoria

So many times, she swam in dark places,
afraid to dive in an inconsistent world.
Pained by love, she removed all traces,
atonement was given to a frightened girl.
She floated above a surface of calories,
undercurrents of self-destructive lies.
Punishment from within, she believed,
hurt less, than love that was disguised.
To fade away in a euphoria of restriction,
an all-consuming, blissful kind of high.
Or, drown in a tidal wave of rejection,
either way, her broken heard finally died.
Too much force from every direction,
pulling her under, holding her down.
Gasping for air, amongst the deception,
she asked "is it best to swim or drown?"

Debra McLain

A Mindless Patter

Chartreuse mountains of clouded fountains
where the purple ship sails horizon bound.
Fitting seas for the gentle solar breezes;
the forgotten found there sleeping sound.

Adrift through your days in a splintered haze;
stolen within the dreams of a mindless patter.
Seeking revenge for life's unforgiving ways;
enchanting breath bestowed by your master.

The ship steers clean and handles so well,
from beyond a tangerine tempest batters;
off in the distance witness the ringing bell
leaving us stifled, wounded and shattered.

Lashed to the rail, driving a breaching whale
into waterless streams of steamy icy mists.
The mind doesn't care, or perhaps won't dare,
to revive and decree the injustice or bliss.

I can't feel the pain through disheartened disdain;
exploring my path while dishonoring all wrath.
I seek a reprieve to a maddened soulless reign;
a lost purple fantasy or wandering psychopath.

Ken Allan Dronsfield

Broken

The words he said left an echo which has only now, begun to fade. "I didn't break you, you were already broken." It felt like a hundred pins were stuck into me all at once, with my body's gating mechanism shut down so that I could feel the pain in every cell of every part of my body. He broke my heart, but it was my whole body which fell apart.

"Broken"- he called me. I was damaged, damaged goods with no value. I spent a long time trying to make sense of that word. A little longer, I spent on anyone who could fix-broken. God, I hated that word.

I wish I could say- that I realized the words he spoke that night were false, lies and nothing more but I can't. I'm only just now learning, maybe he was right; maybe I am broken; but I am so done waiting around for him to come and fix me.

Ameena K.G

Secrets

Many of us carry a secret.
Shame leads us into deeper regret.
Some of us carry more than one.
Cover it up, to hide from the sun.
The longer we hide it the heavier it grows.
Yet still we conceal it, so that nobody knows.
Don't want to remember the secret we hide.
It's always there churning, at our inside.
Substance abuse covers it up for a while.
Who wants to live, with that mad crocodile?
We begin to ruin everything that we touch.
Don't even know, it's not helping that much.
As time passes, we think we forget what we hide,
becomes a dark creature who returns like a tide.
Our selfish destruction pushes loved ones away.
We convince ourselves, we don't care what they say.
If we admit, we are helpless and out of control.
We can attempt to clean our body and soul.
We make a commitment, to prevent our relapse.
Maybe the way is to reveal our secret at last.

Valormore De Plume

Echoes From The Past Repeat

Sharing feelings that here be written,
Gently flow from a soul that's oft been smitten.
To all who's hearts feel bruised or crushed,
Make it arduous, again to trust.
From deep within our heart there be,
A new and different way to see,
the love surrounding you and me.
Release the wrongs we tightly hold,
to feel the joyful peace unfold.
Focus not on troubling doubts,
maddening crowds with angry shouts.
Arise we now on stumbling feet,
as echoes from the past repeat.
Instead, tune in to tender thoughts,
about the things we feel we've lost.
What lies beneath the surface tension
are treasures, surely worth a mention.
A greater love, a greater joy,
a greater hope, we can employ.
To lift our spirits and free our minds,
to leave the troubling thoughts behind.
Take flight onto courageous wings,
take hold of what our wisdom brings.
Allow our open eyes behold,
the love surrounding us unfold.
Cling tight to truthful boundless love,
raining down on us from up above.
Never ending, never cold,
always there for us to hold.

Valormore De Plume

Epilogue

Publishing Assistance

In 2013 Ms. Raja Williams realized that there was a gap, a void if you will, within the publishing industry. A writer either had to come up with hundreds, sometimes thousands of dollars to release a book or take on the journey of self-publishing alone. There was no middle ground, no one there to assist, either financially or lead the way in self-publishing. Most writers do not have the finances to pay a publisher, and some don't know where to start when it comes to self-publishing, nor are they prepared to be in business for themselves.

Raja was inspired to start a fund to assist writers in becoming published authors at either a discounted rate or a full publishing scholarship. To begin this fund Raja paid for the publishing of our first anthology Love, a Four Letter Word. Comprised of poets from all around the world. The sales generated from the purchases of the book were placed into a fund that enabled us to fund future publishing's.

We now are able to offer anthology publications, a chance for authors to have a voice in the literary world yearly, and we have been able to offer several authors full scholarships, as well as offering deep discounted publishing services as a whole. We are thankful for the continued support of this program by both our readers and writers alike.

For More Information Please Visit Our Website At:

www.ctupublishinggroup.com/starving-artist-fund.html

Creative Talents Unleashed

Get Connected With Us!

Website: Creative Talents Unleashed Publishing Group

www.ctupublishinggroup.com

Facebook: Get connected with us on our Facebook Page

www.Facebook.com/Creativetalentsunleashed

Twitter: https://twitter.com/CTUPublishing

Blog: www.creativetalentunleashed.com

Pinterest: https://www.pinterest.com/creativetalents/

Instagram: https://instagram.com/ctupublishinggroup/

Tumblr: http://creativetalentsunleashed.tumblr.com/

Creative Talents Unleashed

Creative Talents Unleashed is an independent publishing group that offers writers an opportunity to share their writing talents with the world. We are committed to fostering and honoring the work of writers of all cultures. Our publishing group offers writing tips to assist writers in continued growth and learning, daily writing prompts and challenges to keep the writers mind sharp and challenged, marketing and events, as well as a variety of yearly publishing opportunities. We are honored to be assisting writers in the journey of becoming published authors.

www.ctupublishinggroup.com

For More Information Contact:

info@ctupublishinggroup.com

www.ingramcontent.com/pod-product-compliance
Lightning Source LLC
Chambersburg PA
CBHW071327040426
42444CB00009B/2104